ABC Florida

Adriane Doherty | Kirsten Halvorsen

Rubber Ducky Press
Indianapolis, Indiana

Aa is for Aquarium.
The colorful fish swimming through the water are so much fun to watch!

Bb is for Bucket.
Let's build a sandcastle!

Cc is for Crab.
I walk sideways along the sandy shore.

Dd is for Dolphins.
Watch them leap above the water!

Ee is for Everglades.
The alligators rule the swamp.

Ff is for Flamingos.
These long-legged pink birds
like to rest on one leg.

Gg is for Gardens. Colorful nature surrounds us everywhere we look.

Hh is for Heat.
Let's cool down at the beach.

Ii is for Island.
This hidden gem is a great place to go fishing.

Jj is for Jellyfish.
We wiggle our way through the water.

Kk is for **K**eys.
Come visit the keys
for food, fun, and
sun!

Ll is for Lobster.
I call the coral reef my home.

Mm is for Manatee. Sometimes this gentle mammal is called a sea cow.

Nn is for Northern Mockingbirds. These Florida birds love to sing.

Oo is for Oranges. Squeeze them for a tasty drink!

Pp is for Pelican.
I can scoop up lots
of fish with my
special beak.

Qq is for Quality time. Playing at the beach is always fun with a friend.

Rr is for Rainbow.
Beautiful colors that stretch
across the Florida sky.

Ss is for Starfish.
Their fun shape is where they get their name.

Tt is for Turtles.
They swim gracefully through the water.

Uu is for Sea Urchin. A spiky shell helps protect this little sea creature.

Vv is for Vacation.
Making memories that
last a lifetime.

Ww is for Waves.
The ripples of water push sea shells onto the shore.

Xx is for X marks the spot. Come back and see us real soon!

Yy is for Yacht.
Gliding across the open gulf, we see a dolphin jumping beside us!

Zz is for Zoo.
I love to splash water
high above my head.

Aa Bb Cc Dd Ee

Ff Gg Hh Ii Jj Kk

Ll Mm Nn Oo Pp

Qq Rr Ss Tt Uu

Vv Ww Xx Yy Zz

Where in Florida did we go today?

The Florida Aquarium, located in Tampa, is home to many aquatic animals. Inside, learn about different habitats, underwater animals, and ways to help keep our planet clean.

Beaches are great for those looking for some fun in the sun! Florida has over 1,300 miles of coastline so there are lots of beaches to choose from.

The Everglades are wetlands and home to a variety of animals. Take a bike ride along the trails, explore the national park, or take a ride on an air boat.

Islands are everywhere! Out of the 50 states, Florida has the second most islands with 4,510.

The Sunken Gardens are full of tropical plants and flowers. Inside, visitors can walk the paths, join a local event, and watch grazing flamingos.

The Florida Keys are made up of hundreds of islands! Take the seven mile bridge across the water to explore the land. Families can enjoy beach days, watch animals play, go fishing, and even scuba dive!

Zoo Miami is the biggest and oldest zoo in Florida. Visit all the animals from gorillas to tigers, toucans to frogs, and so many more. Don't forget to take a river ride while you're there!

Tallahassee is the state capital of Florida, which is also known as The Sunshine State.

Travel to new places with Rubber Ducky Press!

ABC Indiana | ABC Ohio | ABC Michigan

ABC Texas | ABC Yellowstone | ABC Kentucky

ABC Pennsylvania | Sweet Dreams Indiana

Sweet Dreams Ohio | Sweet Dreams Chicago

Sweet Dreams Chesapeake Bay | Wake Up, Woods

One Tomato | Purple Carrot | Chicken & Moodles

Tongue Twisters That Teach

About the Author

Author **Adriane Doherty** has traveled to multiple states to learn about different communities, cultures, and lifestyles. These trips inspire her writing. With her books, Adriane aims to encourage young readers to go on adventures of their own! Shop more titles at www.rubberduckypress.com.

Find printable activity and coloring pages online at www.rubberduckypress.com!

Distributed by Cardinal Publishers Group